Library of
Davidson College

FATHERHOOD AND MOTHERHOOD
IN
ISRAELITE AND JUDEAN PIETY

FATHERHOOD AND MOTHERHOOD IN ISRAELITE AND JUDEAN PIETY

BY

P. A. H. DE BOER

LEIDEN
E. J. BRILL
1974

ISBN 90 04 04159 1

Copyright 1974 by E. J. Brill, Leiden, Netherlands

All rights reserved. No part of this book may be reproduced or translated in any form, by print, photoprint, microfilm, microfiche or any other means without written permission from the publisher

PRINTED IN THE NETHERLANDS

*To the Mother
of my Children*

CONTENTS

Preface IX

Introduction 1
Family 3
Father-God 14
Mother-Goddess 26
God: Father and Mother 38
Genesis I. A Translation 49
Epilogue 52

Index 54
a) Biblical and other references 54
b) Authors cited 56

PREFACE

The text of this monograph reproduces the *Haskell Lectures*, which I had the privilege of delivering at Oberlin College in the spring of 1974. I am happy to be able to express here my deep appreciation of the invitation and the generous hospitality and inspiring fellowship which I received from the Chairman of the Haskell Lectureship Committee, Professor Harry Thomas Frank, his colleagues, their families, and several students throughout the very happy ten days which I spent in their midst.

I have revised some passages and added notes to the lectures. But I did not change their character hoping to hold the attention of a larger circle than students of the history of religion only. A translation of the creation stories from Genesis may make the argument of the fourth lecture clearer.

In conclusion, my warm thanks are due to friends from abroad for improvement of the language, and to the publisher for producing this booklet so well.

Oegstgeest, Leiden P. A. H. DE BOER
August 1974

INTRODUCTION

Dealing with a phenomenon of the religion of ancient Israel means exegesis of the literature of Israelite and Judean origin, handed down to us in the Bible and in a small number of non-biblical texts, and comparison with conceptions preserved in the literature of the ancient Near East. Next to texts figurines and cultic objects contribute to our knowledge of ancient culture and religion.

Fatherhood and Motherhood are an aspect of Israelite piety. A peculiar feature of being engaged in one aspect of a culture and a religion, whose sources are limited, is the danger of a pile of related problems: everything seems to be connected with and even dependent upon a lot of other factors. The whole complexity of a past only partially known and, as regards the Old Testament, of a literature which has reached us through the prism of the rabbis and early Christians with their own intentions, experiences and expectations, —it is all a real difficulty. Too long we have tried to write the history of the religion of ancient Israel as if Israel were the central and focal point of the ancient Near East, and as if the only approach lay through the Judean understanding of God's purpose in creating the world and mankind. The Bible takes a prominent role in our own religion. I deem it high time that we should distinguish the Judeo-Christian presupposition to be found in the texts handed down to us as "Holy Scriptures" from what we know through exegesis. The latter should determine our attempts to justify the role of the Old and New Testament in our religious practice.

Although I will try to limit myself to the subject, Fatherhood and Motherhood in Israelite and Judean piety, I cannot avoid some aspects of larger scope, nor some problems of our own spiritual situation. However, it is good to bear in mind that our subject is no more than one aspect of religious life.

FAMILY

Wat eenzaam leeft is levend dood
Joost van den Vondel

Reaching manhood, womanhood, marriage, child-birth, fatherhood, motherhood, maintenance of the family, authority in the family—these all belong to the elementary and essential matters of life. It seems certain that Israel, in its relatively short period of existence as a more or less independent people in Palestine, shared the patriarchal standard of society with surrounding cultures. Men held a superior position.

Ben Sira, whose collection of instructions for life dates from *circa* 200 B.C., states—and his word is often quoted—"From a woman sin had its beginning, and because of her we all die".[1] Eve was the first to eat from the fruit of the tree of total knowledge. The knowledge of good and evil brought man and woman into life's reality characterized by life and death, pain, desire, domination, and hard labour—the story of the Garden in Eden, the lost paradise.[2]

Philo portrayed Sarah, Abraham's wife, with words the very opposite to ben Sira's valuation of woman, "... a wife distinguished greatly for her goodness of soul and beauty of body, in which she surpassed all the women of her time".[3] This picture reflects the Greek ideal image of woman and concurs with a line of the Genesis Apocryphon from Qumran: "Yet with all this beauty there is much wisdom in her".[4]

Wisdom, *ḥokmah*, described as a woman, is to be loved. "I loved her more than health and beauty", says the author of the

---

[1] xxv 24.
[2] Gen. iii.
[3] *de Abrahamo* par. 93.
[4] Column xx, line 7. Cf. J. A. Fitzmyer, *The Genesis Apocryphon of Qumran Cave I*, A Commentary, Rome 1966, pp. 55, 110.

Wisdom of Solomon.[5] "All good things come to me along with her, and in her hands is uncounted wealth. .... but I did not know that she was their mother"—in a recent translation: "—and I was in ignorance before, that she is in the beginning of it all".[6]

In the Book of Proverb wisdom is also personified.[7] She is a Lady with an important function in the ordering or creation of the world. In chapter iii of Proverbs [8] she is praised with terms similar to the words in the Wisdom of Solomon. "Happy is the man who finds wisdom—for length of days are in her right hand, in her left wealth and honour". "She is a tree of life" (producing the conditions for life). By wisdom the Lord founded the earth. In chapter viii of Proverbs she is pictured as a counsellor. The Lord acquires [9] her at the beginning of his works, his undertaking to create heaven and earth. Wisdom exists prior to the creative acts of the Lord. She is called "the most primaeval of his acts in antiquity"; [10] or "a counsellor", like the queen-mother at the royal court.[11]

The text runs as follows,[12]

"When he established the heavens, I was there,
when he drew a circle on the face of the deep,

---

[5] vii 10 ff.
[6] The New English Bible. Further abbreviated as NEB.
[7] viii 22-31.
[8] iii 13-20.
[9] The Hebrew verb *qnh* is rendered here with "to acquire" in view of the statement that Wisdom's origin lies far back in time before the creative acts of the Lord. To acquire wisdom, Prov. iv 5, a.o., is a usual expression. Cf. my "The Councellor", *Supplements to Vetus Testamentum* III, 1955, reprint 1969, p. 69 f. The traditional rendering is "to create", cf. W. McKane, *Proverbs*, London 1970, p. 352; G. von Rad, *Weisheit in Israel*, Neukirchen-Vluyn 1970, p. 198 (ET *Wisdom in Israel*, Londen 1972).
[10] McKane, *o.c.* p. 223.
[11] Cf. H. Ringgren, *Word and Wisdom*. Studies in the Hypostatization of Divine Qualities and Functions in the Ancient Near East, Lund 1947, p. 99 f; also my "The Counsellor", *a.c.*
[12] Prov. viii 27-31.

when he made firm the skies above,
when he established (?) the fountains of the deep,
when he assigned to the sea its limit,
so that the waters might not transgress his command,
when he marked out the foundations of the earth,
then I was beside him, a beloved little mother,
and I was daily a [13] delight,
merry before him always,
sporting in the world, his earth,
and my delights with the sons of man".

"Beloved little mother" is a rendering of the Hebrew '*mwn*, read as '*immôn*, a hypocoristicon for '*ēm*, mother, possibly a love-name for the beloved and inspiring consort.[14] Wisdom, merry, making sport before the Lord, is a remarkable line of this wonderful poem of which is said "a fleeting suggestion of marital joys".[15]

Sarah's portrait and the picture of Wisdom are in sharp contrast indeed with ben Sira's "Woman is the origin of sin and it is through her that we all die".[16] It is wrong to derive from ben Sira's words a dogma on women's wickedness. Scholars like Hamp and Marböck [17] rightly point to ben Sira's eulogy on intelligent wives: "Happy is the husband of a good wife,[18] she is a great blessing, she will be granted among the blessings of the man who fears the Lord".[19] But on the whole it must be stated

---

[13] In the Greek rendering: his (delight).
[14] "The Counsellor", *a.c.* p. 70. The masoretic reading of the consonantal text is '*āmôn*, a term which has got a series of translations: architect, nurse, little child, master workman, etc. Cf. R. B. Y. Scott, in *Vetus Testamentum* X 1960, p. 213 ff.
[15] E. H. Lantero, *Feminine Aspects of Divinity*, Pendle Hill Pamphlet 191, Philadelphia 1973.
[16] Rendering of the NEB.
[17] V. Hamp, "Paradis und Tod" in *Festschrift J. Schmid*, Regensburg 1963; J. Marböck, *Weisheit im Wandel*, Bonn 1971, p. 152 f.
[18] xxvi 1.
[19] xxv 13-26.

that a negative valuation of woman dominates both in Jewish and in Christian writings. Woman was given to Adam to glorify his life, *or*, for an advisor, but she counselled him, *or*, she played the eavesdropper, like a serpent, says a rabbinic midrash. Also in public worship man claimed a superior position: There existed a temple court for women, second class; a prayer of thanks not to be born as a woman;[20] and a Christian rule for worship from about the same time as rabbi Jehudah's saying:

> "I permit no woman to teach or to have authority over men; she is to keep silent. For Adam was formed first, then Eve; and Adam was not deceived, but the woman—ἡ δὲ γυνὴ—was deceived and became a transgressor".[21]

From this rule arose a "stabilized piety" which has maintained itself up to the present time in a number of denominations. "Here is a case", says Morgan P. Noyes, "where an early Christian's understanding of the will of God needs to be corrected...".[22]

There are many instances of subordination of women to men. Women, wives, daughters, are regarded as of minor importance and put into subservient relation to men, husbands, fathers. A wife calls her husband "master", *baʻal*; "lord" *ʼādôn*; similarly a daughter her father *ʼādôn*. In the Decalogue the wife is placed in the same category as house, male and female slaves, ox, ass and everything belonging to the husband. A rule on special vows, transmitted in a rather late text, runs as follows,[23]

> "The Lord said to Moses, 'Say to the people of Israel, When a man makes a special vow of persons to the Lord

---

[20] First assigned to rabbi Jehudah ben Elay, circa 150 A.D.; a similar saying is preserved in Greek texts; quotations in J. Leipoldt, *Jesus und die Frauen*, Leipsic 1921.
[21] 1 Timothy ii 11-14.
[22] The Interpreter's Bible, 1955, p. 407.
[23] Lev. xxvii 1ff.

at your valuation (an expression which can be paraphrased, when anyone fulfills a vow of offering one or more persons to the Lord, who are to be ransomed at a fixed sum of money,[24]) then your valuation of a male from twenty years old up to sixty years old shall be fifty shekels of silver, according to the shekel of the sanctuary. If the person is a female, your valuation shall be thirty shekels".

In general, women, wife and mother are ranked second. It remains open to discussion whether they kept the same valuation in ancient Israel and pre-exilic Judah. Women can have special rights, in particular the mothers. She is the one to name her child in twenty-five cases, as against the father in eighteen cases.[25] In late texts assigned to priestly writers it is always the father who names the child. The most usual form of marriage must have been that of the woman taking up her residence with the family of the man. The married woman and the children born from this marriage belong to the authority and the protection of the father of her husband. But from the expression "to come to the woman" Plautz, in the article referred to, derives a matrilocal marriage. Mace points at the tendency in polygamy to foster strong ties of loyalty among children of the same mother. The mother appears to be the centre in special groups within the family.[26] The religious ceremonies are confined to males. When Moses in the exodus story asks permission to go in the desert for a few days to hold a religious feast with their families, flocks and herds, Pharaoh only admits the adult men to go. The used term *ṭaph*, small children, sometimes covers the mothers as well.[27]

---

[24] NEB.
[25] Cf. W. Plautz on the rights of the mother in *ZAW* 74, 1962 "Monogamie und Polygamie im Alten Testament", p. 9 ff. His thesis, *Die Frau in Ehe und Familie*, Ein Beitrag zum Problem ihrer Stellung im Alten Testament, Kiel 1959, is as far as I know not published.
[26] D. R. Mace, London 1953, a sociological study on *Hebrew Marriage*.
[27] See D. Daube, *The Exodus Pattern in the Bible*, London 1963, chapter VI, Family and Cattle, p. 47 ff. Ex. x 7 ff.

Fatherhood and motherhood are considered to be essential for happiness. At the end of life consolidation with the family is aimed at. Disaster befalls the man who is not buried in the grave of his fathers.[28] Abraham asks the Hittites, in whose region he is living, to sell him a property for a burying place, that he may remove [29] his dead, his wife Sarah. He is a long-term resident but still a "sojourner and settler", lacking the privilege of a citizen, the right to own land. Husband and wife are to remain united, also in death. Not because of romantism or sentiment but because of the blessing for their children, the family.

A kinship group was considerably wider in its binding ties than the modern Western family. This group was called *bēt-ʼāb*, "house of the father", and comprises three generations.[30] *ʼōhel*, tent, may be called the ancient name for *bēt-ʼāb*. Life was centred in the tent. *ʼōhel* is a term occurring in almost every Semitic language.[31] The term indicates both dwelling and its inhabitants. Tent points to periodical movement, migration, necessary for the sustenance of life, the way of living of nomads and semi-nomads. The term remained in use during the settled existence. The plural form of the word, *ʼōhālîm*, serves to indicate peoples, "the tents of Edom and Moab are the descendants of Ishmael and Hagar";[32] "the tents of Jacob",[33] and "the tents of Judah",[34] the Israelites and the Judeans.

---

[28] Cf. Johs Pedersen, *Israel, its life and culture*, III/IV, p. 478 f: "If a man dies at a ripe age, surrounded by his family, he passes precisely to those forefathers who are the upholders of the blessing. For him as for the family it is then important that the normal fellowship should be preserved, and this takes place through the burial".

[29] Remove, translation of E. A. Speiser, *Anchor Bible*, 1964. Gen. xxiii 4.

[30] Cf. J. R. Porter, *The extended family in the Old Testament*, London 1967, p. 7. *bēt-ʼāb* by the time of Ezra-Nehemiah *bēt-ʼābōt*, cf. J. P. Weinberg, *VT* XXIII, 1973, 400 ff.

[31] See K. Koch, *s.v.* in *Theol. Wörterbuch zum Alten Testament*, Stuttgart 1971.

[32] Ps. lxxxiii 7.

[33] Jer. xxx 18.

[34] Zech. xii 7.

Urbanization changed the forms of life.³⁵ Palestine did not have large towns. There were a number of small towns which formed together with their surroundings a more or less independent state, a πόλις, on which the El Amarna letters give some information. It is not primarily urbanization, in my opinion, that pushed back the central place of families, the kinship groups in the Israelite society in Palestine. Towns in the Near East, big and small ones, have been marked until the present day by the living together of families in units, blocs, which are rather difficult to survey. Handicraft used to be connected to families, also in towns. In my opinion the concentration of power by kings is the first cause of the diminishing influence of the family. The royal court, a standing army, royal tribute, diplomacy and commerce brought about the changes in social life. The king is in principle different from the sheik. "These will be the ways of the king who will reign over you,

> he will take your sons —
> he will take your daughters —
> he will take the best of your fields —
> he will take the tenth of your grain —
> he will take your slaves, male and female, the elite of your young men, and your asses,
> and make them his property".³⁶

The royal property includes servants, fields, cattle, court, just as does the property of a wealthy family. But the royal property is required, recruited from the families. Moreover, the king's court and his standing commanders, and everyone to whom the king grants favours, are influenced by the booty of expeditions, women as female slaves and concubines, cattle, gold, silver.

---

³⁵ I wish to mention here Horst Klengel's well documented study, *Zwischen Zelt und Palast*, Leipsic 1971.

³⁶ 1 Sam. viii 11-16, the conduct of an authority, *mishpāṭ* of the king. "and make them his property", see my contribution to *Festschrift M. A. Beek*, Assen, 1974, p. 27 ff.

Diplomacy and commerce bring foreigners with their customs, culture and religion into the towns of the king. The royal property seems to be the most important cause of the regression of independency of family and tribe.

This opinion about the changing social situation in ancient Israel seems to be supported by the description of the opposite situation, the ruin of royal power. Ruin of royal power is expressed by the return of the soldiers and servants to their ancestral families. After Absalom's death it is said, "And all Israel fled everyone to his tent".[37] The renderings, "to his own home",[38] "to their homes"[39] are correct explanations, *'ōhel*, tent, indicates *bayit*, home. But these renderings miss the ancient flavour. Sheba, a kinsman of Saul, a member of the Benjamite clan, made a bold attempt to revive the Israelite kingdom, against David.[40] He blew the trumpet and said,

> "We have no portion in David,
> and we have no inheritance in Jesse's son,
> every man to his tents, O Israel!"

And after Rehoboam's harsh answer, forsaking the counsel which the elders had given him, the Israelites under the leadership of Jeroboam said,[41]

> "What portion have we in David?
> We have no inheritance in Jesse's son.
> To your tents, O Israel!"

The rule of David's dynasty over the centre and the north of Palestine, over Israel, came to an end.

When Amaziah, king of Judah, tried to conquer Israel, wishing to restore David's empire, he was defeated by Jehoash,

---

[37] 2 Sam. xviii 17b; comp. too xix 8b.
[38] The Revised Standard Version. Further abbreviated as RSV.
[39] NEB.
[40] 2 Sam. xx 1.
[41] 1 Kings xii 16.

king of Israel, in a battle at Beth-Shemesh.⁴² "And every man fled to his tent", is said about Amaziah's soldiers.

It was the beginning of a real ruin of Amaziah's kingdom. The conqueror captured Judah's king, broke down a part of the wall of his capital-town, Jerusalem, and seized the treasures of both the temple and the palace. In such calamities people fall back on the ancient structure of life, the family.

The family—manhood, womanhood, marriage, child-birth, fatherhood, motherhood, maintenance of the family, authority in the family, respect to the forefathers. The consistent and serious interest in genealogy during the period after the fall of dynasty and kingdom, the exilic and post-exilic period without independency and security, might be connected with the need of identity and safety. In priestly circles strong emphasis was laid on establishing the continuity of pre-exilic Israel and the post-exilic Judean community. The genealogical form was used in a variety of ways, "une oeuvre d'art" (Lefèvre), used "above all for apologetic purposes, both nationalistic and theological" (Johnson).⁴³

Even the Levites need a kinship group, a family. The sanctuaries to which the Levite belonged, situated in the region of a tribe which was, or could be, other than his own, were changed or became ruined, and even the restored temple in Jerusalem did not guarantee a secure life nor any acknowledgment. The Levite, of whom was said,⁴⁴

"who said of his father and mother,
I regard them not,
who disowned his brothers
and ignored his children . . .",

---

[42] 2 Kings xiv 8-14.
[43] See M. D. Johnson, *The Purpose of the Biblical Genealogies with special reference to the setting of the genealogies of Jesus*, Cambridge 1969, in particular p. 71-82. Johnson's reference to A. Lefèvre's article in *Recherches de Sciences Religieuses* 37 1950, on p. 71 and 73.
[44] Deuter. xxxiii 9.

is now looking for his own identity. The history of the post-exilic temple in Jerusalem is a chain of strife, priestly families quarreling to gain supremacy, and degradation of the weak groups. The accepted conception of the origin of a separate tribe of Levi might stem from that difficult period.[45] Proof of identity would be their descent from the forefather Jacob. There are no arguments for a secular tribe of Levi in the ancient texts. The picture of the family story of the forefather Jacob with twelve sons might contain some old items, it should not be considered to be a historical record of the past.[46] Its meaning lies elsewhere.

To be without a family is to be without security, without rights and protection, without a future. Orphan and widow depend on the king. The woman of Tekoa, going to the king, can be assured of David's help by saying, "I am a widow". King Karit in the Ugaritic legend judges the cause of the widow, he has to feed orphan and widow.[47] And king Danel, also a Ugaritic monarch, judges the cause of the widow and tries the case of the orphan.[48] Isaiah's oracle [49] contains as well as the Lord's despising of offerings, cultic feasts and prayers, a series of commands and among them, "defend the fatherless, plead for the widow". God himself is mentioned as "a father of the fatherless", and "protector (judge) of widows".[50] "He executes justice for the fatherless and the widow, and loves the sojourner, giving him food and clothes".[51]

Loneliness, to be a stranger, is misery. A person banished from his family is an exile: ex solis > exsul patria. "Woe is me,

---

[45] Cf. Johnson, *o.c.* p. 71 ff.
[46] Cf. my *Gods beloften over land en volk in het Oude Testament*, Delft 1955; and the recent important study of Th. L. Thompson, *The Historicity of the Patriarchal Narratives*, *BZAW* 133, Berlin 1974.
[47] Krt II vi 45 ff.
[48] Aqht II v 6 ff.
[49] Isa. i 12-17.
[50] Ps. lxviii 6.
[51] Deuter. x 18.

my mother, that you bore me", complains Jeremiah, feeling himself an outcast,[52] "a man of strife and contention to the whole land. I did not sit in the company of merrymakers, nor did I rejoice; I sat alone because thy hand was upon me, for thou hadst filled me with indignation".[53] A psalmist in a miserable situation compares himself to a bird of the wilderness, to an owl of the waste places, a lonely bird on the roof.[54]

Belonging to a family is a condition for life. It is no matter of surprise to find epithets of God borrowed from the relationship in the kinship group.

---

[52] Jer. xv 10.
[53] xv 17.
[54] Ps. cii 7 f. Comp. Pedersen, *o.c.* I, p. 263, "Loneliness the lack of community the Old Testament only knows as something unnatural, an expression that life is failing."

FATHER-GOD

saevit quantum vult, pater est
Augustin

In the first phase of our life father and mother are central figures, each in his or her own way and also both together. They withdraw from our lives as we develop and attain more independence and our experiences happen outside the privacy of the family. This second phase of our life, however, is often characterized by the fact that we ourselves become a father, a mother. When during the last phase of life the urge towards going our own ways and possibilities of doing so diminish, we put ourselves questions like: how was I prepared for life, physically and psychically, when I began my life? What has been my own creation, my children, my work, what has been brought to maturity by me? Who and what do I leave behind? Fatherhood and motherhood become again, now in a more contemplative way, important.

In our days dependence on our family is no longer considered to be an essential good. Both father and mother strive for more independence and the education of our children is directed to an early self-supporting life. It is true that the evolution of our social life, of the economy, of political and states affairs, business and relaxation, of science and also in ideological philosophic systems, points more at a growth of collectivism than of individualism. But the diminishing of our personal freedom has not increased the privacy and intimacy of our family life.

Through this the religious practice of using names like father, mother, son, daughter, brother, sister has become more or less isolated, a kind of religious language, to compare with the language used in our translations of the Bible. In an age when our Dad is already for a long time—if everything goes well, and we still have a father—our friend, we pray to God as our

Father who is in heaven, and we are his children. The religious language seems to continue our child world, adults using children language.

"Our Father who art in heaven" is a frequently used title of God, in Jewish and in Christian piety. The title is derived from the Old Testament but its application to Yhwh, the Lord, is less frequent than we would suppose. The relation of the king and his god has been expressed by the term, the son and his father, but only in a very limited number of texts.[1] Individual addresses wherein God is called "my father", "your, his father" are very rare.

In a Sumerian wisdom text [2] we find,

"My god, you are my father who begot me—".

In the Old Testament and in Semitic Inscriptions [3] a number of personal names occur which contain "my father" as part of the name indicating God's protection. "My father, thou art the friend (confidant) of my youth" [4] is no individual expression. The line deals with the inhabitants of Judah, pictured as the Lord's wife.[5] We have to turn up ben Sira's book to find more examples of God as father in the sayings of individual believers,

κύριε πάτερ καὶ δέσποτα ζωῆς μου
"O Lord, Father and Ruler of my life" [6]

κύριε πάτερ καὶ θεὲ ζωῆς μου
"O Lord, Father and God of my life" [7]

continuing with a prayer for protection.

---

[1] 2 Sam. vii 14a; Ps. lxxxix 27 f; 1 Chron. xxviii 6, 9; Ps. ii 7.
[2] S. N. Kramer described the text as a variation of the "Job" motive, see *The Ancient Near East, Supplementary materials to ANET*, 1969, p. 589 ff.
[3] Cf. H. Ringgren, in *ThWAT*, s.v. ʾāb, Stuttgart 1970, and J. C. L. Gibson, *Textbook of Syrian Semitic Inscriptions*, Oxford 1971, p. 102.
[4] Jer. iii 4, 19.
[5] Similarly the subject is collective in Deuter. xxxii 6; Mal. i 6; ii 10.
[6] xxiii 1. *Sapientia Iesu Filii Sirach*, ed. J. Ziegler, Göttingen 1965.
[7] xxiii 4.

The Hebrew text of ben Sira li 10, which is clearer than the Greek version, reads,

"I appeal to the Lord, my Father art thou,
my God and the Fighter (*gibbôr*, soldier, hero) for my salvation".

In a prayer from Qumran [8] we read the same, individually used, titles "my father" and "my mother" applied to God,

"My father does not concern himself with me
and in comparison with you my mother has left me,
but you are father of all thy faithfull
and you rejoiced at those like a loving mother at her infant
and like a foster-father you cherish in your bosom all your creatures".

The individual speaker is here praying as a member of the community.

A non-literal use of the term father (and mother) occurs both outside and within Israel. Kilamuwa, a king of a land in North Syria, praises the domestic accomplishments he made.[9] His inscription dates from *circa* 825 B.C. He says to have improved the position of the conquered native population, the *mūshkābîn*, probably the farmers of the land now in king Kilamuwa's power. I quote some lines of the inscription,

"to some I was a father. To some I was a mother. To some I was a brother".

His treatment of those people like a father, mother, brother appears to be that he provided them with sheep, cattle, silver, gold and clothes.

---

[8] 1QH ix 35 f.
[9] Cf. M. Lidzbarski, *Ephemeris für semitische Epigraphik* III, Giessen 1915, p. 218 ff; F. Rosenthal, in *Ancient Near Eastern Texts relating to the Old Testament (ANET)*, sec. ed. 1955, p. 500 f; H. Donner-W. Röllig, *Kanaanäische Inschriften (KAI)*, third ed. Texte 1971, Kommentar 1973; No. 24.

'Azitawadda, king of the Danunites, left a bilingual Phoenician-Hittite inscription, dated *circa* 720 B.C.[10] The king records that his God Ba'al made him a father and a mother to the Danunites. In his time the population had plenty of food and the strength of his government was secured. He made peace with every king. "Yea, every king considered me his father [11] because of my righteousness and my wisdom and the kindness of my heart". The authority of the father includes justice, wisdom and kindness.

Hammurabi (1728-1686) is named "the lord, who is like a real father to the people" in the epilogue to his Code.[12]

Let us deal now with the Old Testament instances.

In Isaiah xxii a story is told about two stewards of the king in Jerusalem. King Hezekiah's steward Shebna, "who is over the household", is criticized, on behalf of the Lord. He loses his post. Eliakim becomes his successor. We are told, "And he shall be a father to the inhabitants of Jerusalem and to the house of Judah. And I—i.e. the Lord—will put the key of David's house on his shoulder, and he shall open and none shall shut, and he shall shut and none shall open".[13] This steward is called a servant of the Lord, verse 20. His fatherhood for the inhabitants is derived from God whose servant he is.

Jerusalem's sons and daughters, the inhabitants of the city, are qualified as "whom you—the city as wife of the deity—have borne to me", to the Lord.[14] And in a text, which reminds them of the educative concern of the father, "sons have I reared and brought up",[15] a prophet is reproaching the people: "For they

---

[10] *ANET*², p. 499 f and *Suppl.* p. 653 f; *KAI* No. 26A.
[11] "his father", translation of Rosenthal; Donner-Röllig read *b'bt*: "sogar zur Vaterschaft erwählte (machte) mich jeder König wegen meiner Gerechtigkeit und wegen meiner Weisheit und wegen der Güte meines Herzens".
[12] Reverse xxv, line 20.
[13] Isa. xxii 21b, 22.
[14] Ezek. xvi 20.
[15] Isa. i 2.

are a rebellious people, lying sons—literally, disappointing sons—, sons who will not hear the instruction of the Lord".[16]

The term "father" in a non-literal sense is also used for inventors, the first person who made tents to dwell in, who invented the breeding of cattle as a living, the inventor of musical instruments, of sharpening metals for agriculture.

> "Adah bore Jabal; he was the father of those who dwell in tents and have cattle. His brother's name was Jubal; he was the father of all those who play the lyre and pipe. Zillah bore Tubal-Cain; he was the sharpener (whetter) of all instruments of bronze and iron".[17]

We will dwell on the remarkable story in Judges xvii-xviii a bit longer. Micah's mother consecrated two hundred pieces of silver to Yhwh, to make a graven image, a molten image, evidently an image of the Lord. Micah had a shrine and installed one of his sons as his priest, just as David's sons were priests according to 2 Samuel viii 18. A young man, a Judean Levite,[18] having left his father and mother, his family—to refer to the lines on Levi in the song on Jacob's sons in Deuteronomy xxxiii 9—applied for the post of priest. He was accepted by Micah who treated the young man as one of his sons,[19] an expression indicating that the Levite got his food and everything from his patron, like the people at the court of the kings who "ate at the king's table". His dignity as a priest is described as "a father and a priest" to the owner of the sanctuary.[20] The same title is used in chapter xviii 19. The young Judean Levite, "father and priest" to Micah's family, is asked to be "father and

---

[16] Isa. xxx 9.
[17] Gen. iv 20-22.
[18] Judg. xvii 7: "Now there was a young man of Bethlehem in Judah, of the family of Judah, who was a Levite....". There can be no question that the Hebrew text mentions Judah as homeland of the Levite.
[19] xvii 11.
[20] xvii 10.

priest" to the Danites, who stole Micah's image of the Lord, the ephod and the teraphim. The Levite did not refuse; it was something like a promotion of a vicar to a bishopric! It is clear that the term 'father' in this remarkable story does not mean a substitute for the real father. It seems probable, I think, that in the title "father" is expressed the idea that he as a priest represents the Lord whose image and whose worship are the centre of his task at the sanctuary. As a priest the Levite is acting for the Father-God and his title is to be derived from God's fatherhood.

From this view of the meaning of the title "father" it is possible, in my opinion, to understand the difficult text of the Joseph story, Joseph "a father to Pharaoh".[21] Donald B. Redford has convincingly demonstrated [22] that the assumption of an Egyptian title as background of the term is improbable. The text runs as follows,

> "So it was not you—namely Joseph's brothers—who sent me here, but God; and he (God) has made me a father to Pharaoh, and lord of all the house and ruler over all the land of Egypt".

Joseph is representing God to Pharaoh. His appointment has been considered by the pious narrator of the *novelle* as an act of his God. Joseph's becoming viceroy of Egypt,[23] bearer of the royal seal, is not the result of a free act of the Egyptian king. Joseph's wisdom—the principal motive to his appointment as a viceroy—is God's wisdom. Joseph answered Pharaoh: [24] "It is not in me; God will give Pharaoh a favourable answer".

The title "father" is also given to prophets. "Who is their

---

[21] Gen. xlv 8.
[22] *A study of the Biblical story of Joseph, Supplements to VT* XX, Leiden 1970, pp. 191 ff.
[23] Gen. xli 39 ff.
[24] Gen. xli 16. See my "The Counsellor", *a.c.* p. 57 ff.

father?" is asked of a band of prophets.²⁵ Elisha cries to his master Elijah "my father, my father!", and similarly king Joash, visiting Elisha, says "my father, my father!" ²⁶ And the king of Israel also addresses Elisha by "my father".²⁷ This title can be explained, I think, in the same way. The prophet is "a man of God", *'îsh hā-'elōhîm*, in whom the deity appears. Calling him "father" is acknowledging the Fatherhood of the God of the prophet.

A prophet is a man with knowledge given to him through intuition and ecstasy. As late as the times of the Babylonian Talmud intuition was known as the essence of prophecy. Concerning a statement without arguments is said *'āśū dibrē nĕbî'ût*, they made statements, or decisions like prophetic statements, i.e. they did not give motives for their opinions.²⁸ And concerning the skill of Judean people to solve a difficult ritual problem Hillel says *'im 'ēn nĕbî'îm bĕnē nĕbî'îm hēn*, they might be no prophets, they are (at least) sons of prophets, i.e. they shall know by intuition to do what is right.²⁹

A teacher, a wise man, acquires knowledge from tradition and deduction. The latter too is called a "father", and he names his pupils "sons". The Lord himself is pictured as a teacher, "sons have I reared and brought up",³⁰ a text already quoted. "As a man disciplines his son, the Lord your God disciplines you".³¹ And the wise teacher, giving his teaching divine authority, says to his pupil,

> "My son, do not despise the Lord's discipline
> or be weary of his reproof,

---

[25] 1 Sam. x 12.
[26] 2 Kings iii 12; xiii 14.
[27] 2 Kings vi 21.
[28] bBekhorot f. 45a. Quotations from M. Jastrow, *A Dictionary to the Targumim, the Talmud Babli and Yerushalmi and the Midrashic Literature*, London 1903.
[29] bPesachim f. 66a.
[30] Isa. i 2.
[31] Deuter. viii 5.

for the Lord reproves him who he loves
and as a father the son in whom he delights".[32]

A king, a royal steward, a priest, a prophet, a wise man—all of them are outstanding people. Their title "father" appears to be derived from the divine authority behind their position. All of them are called to be a "father", directly or indirectly by the deity. All—except the king who is a successor in a dynasty: he is born a king. The king may be said to be a father, or to be like a father, he himself is referred to as a son of God. The well known text from the Book of Samuel [33] alludes to a dynasty. Concerning David's son Solomon is said,

"I shall be a father to him and he shall be a son to me,
whom I, in case he shall misbehave, will chasten
with a human rod and blows like those that men give".

In Psalm lxxxix, clearly connected with the chapter from the Book of Samuel, David is made the firstborn of the Lord, whose line will be established for ever and whose throne will be as the days of the heavens.[34] Next to these texts only one poetical line is transmitted which speaks of the king of Zion begotten by the Lord, Psalm ii. If the idea of a divine promise concerning the everlasting kingship of David's dynasty should be earlier than Psalm ii, the Lord's decree:

"... I will tell of the decree of the Lord:
he said to me, 'You are my son,
to-day I have begotten you",

would be unnecessary. This points to a late date of the Samuel pericope and of Psalm lxxxix.

Paffrath called attention to some Babylonian monarchs who

---

[32] Prov. iii 12.
[33] 2 Sam. vii 14; partly quoted in 1 Chron. xvii 3.
[34] Ps. lxxxix 21 ff.

name several gods as their father or their mother.³⁵ He thinks it very probable that we have to do with an adoption. The royal child would have been put on the lap of the images of the deity, a ceremony of adoption. Ringgren assumes also a formula of adoption in Ps. ii 7 "You are my son, to-day I have begotten you".³⁶ According to him God as father did not have a central position in the religion of Israel, the image seems to be formed ad hoc. The conception, the king as son of God, however, is more clearly formulated,³⁷ be it rare.

"You are my son" as a formula of adoption is a much accepted interpretation of the second Psalm. In a study on the conception "the son of God in the Old Testament" ³⁸ I have made a marginal note to this explanation. It is true that the Israelites were familiar with adoption, but the right of adoption brings us into an entirely different realm of ideas than that of the kingship. Adoption has to do with the rights of children in a family and such rights are often stipulations concerning inheritance. It is quite clear that such an adoption is not relevant when the king at his coronation is elevated to the status of a son of God.

In early Christian doctrine and piety the son of God is put on a level of equality with God himself. The words from the second Psalm "You are my son" are used in the report concerning Jesus' baptism by John.³⁹ Jesus became the son of God, begotten by God and clothed with supernatural might. In this respect early Christianity continues the conception of divine kingship, possibly influenced by the renaissance of Old Egyptian

---

[35] P. Th. Paffrath, "Der Titel 'Sohn der Gottheit' ", in *Orientalische Studien Fritz Hommel gewidmet* I, Leipsic 1917, p. 157 ff.

[36] *ThWAT* I, 1970. See recently Sir Godfrey R. Driver's important article "King by Divine Adoption", in *Abu Husain: Felicitation Volume*, 1974, p. 15 ff. Driver translates Ps. ii 7 as follows: "—this day have I adopted thee." Comp. the rendering in NEB, "this day I become your father."

[37] "fester geprägt".

[38] *Oudtestamentische Studiën* XVIII, Leiden 1973, p. 188-207.

[39] Matth. iii 17, Mark i 11, Luke iii 22.

conceptions and the complex phenomena of the Hellenistic ideas.[40]

Adoption can cover a wider field than the juridical meaning of the term. The relation of God and king, and through the king of God and people, might have been more popular in ancient Israel's piety than the priestly recension of the texts suggests.[41] Guthrie, writing about the Greeks and their Gods, formulates the ancient ideas of the mysterious union of God and man convincingly: "One form of this union was rebirth, or adoption, as son of the divinity. The two ideas are not separate, for in human families in Greece the solemn adoption of a child was represented as rebirth from the womb of his new mother. Later writers speak of those initiated in certain mysteries .... as "reborn", and this phrase was also applied to adopted children".[42]

Divine kingship is in the Old Testament a very rare idea, contrary to the conception that the Lord is the father of the people. "When Israel was a child, I began to love it", says the prophet Hosea, "from Egypt have I called my son".[43] Israel and Ephraim are Yhwh's firstborn son.[44]

In the Book of Second-Isaiah the conception of the Fatherhood of the Lord is often connected with the creation of man. "Bring my sons from afar and my daughters from the end of the earth, each one of them who bear my name, whom I have created to my glory, whom I both formed and made".[45] In a prayer for deliverance from captivity, alongside a recollection of Jerusalem's desolation, we find the argument: "Now then,

---

[40] It may suffice to refer to studies of S. Morenz, *Religion in Geschichte und Gegenwart*, third ed., s.v. Sohn Gottes; and of E. Schweizer and E. Lohse in *Theol. Wörterbuch zum Neuen Testament* (ET *TDNT*), s.v. *huios*.
[41] See e.g. below, p. 45 ff, on the creation mythes of Gen. i.
[42] W. K. C. Guthrie, *The Greek and their Gods*, London 1962, p. 292. I owe the quotations from Guthrie to Miss C. J. L. Kloos, class. dra.
[43] Hos. xi 1.
[44] Exod. iv 22b, 23; Jer. xxxi 9.
[45] Isa. xliii 6.

O Lord, you are our father; we are the clay and you are the potter; we are all the work of your hand".[46] According to this poet the forefathers in the literal sense are unable to redeem: "Abraham is not concerned about us and Israel does not look at us. You, O Lord, are our father, our redeemer is your name from of old".[47] Jesus too refused the claim to be heir of Abraham, according to the Gospels,[48]

> "Bear fruits that befit repentance
> and do not begin to say to yourselves, 'We have Abraham as our father'; for I tell you, God is able from these stones to raise up children to Abraham".

And Palestine is a land full of stones...

Lagrange emphasized that Israel has not become the son of the Lord by adoption, but rather the people was by birth son of the deity.[49] "Israël ne devient pas fils par adoption étant déjà peuple, et choisi ensuite par Jahvé; c'est Jahvé qui lui a donné d'être, et c'est pour cela qu'il est son père". He refers to Deuteronomy xxxii 6b,

> "Is not he your father, who created you,
> who made you and established you?"

The song preserved in Deuteronomy xxxii might preserve ancient ideas. It is difficult, I think, to distinguish between "birth" and "rebirth", adoption, however. The version handed down to us seems influenced by the prophetic idea of the punishment of the people because of their sins. "Do you thus requite the Lord, you foolish and senseless people?" God's fatherhood implies his right to punish whenever he considers his name to be dishonoured by their behaviour. He is able to

---

[46] Isa. lxiv 7.
[47] Isa. lxiii 16.
[48] Matth. iii 9; Luke iii 8; John viii 33.
[49] "La paternité de Dieu dans l'Ancien Testament", in *Revue Biblique* 1908, p. 481-499.

sell them as slaves. But remembering the days of old might lead to new hope, to a return. The song reflects, in my opinion, the calamities of fall and exile. The only hope is that the Father-God will show himself as the Redeemer. Compare the prayer of post-exilic times,

> "Be not exceedingly angry, O Lord,
> and remember not iniquity for ever.
> Behold, consider, we are all thy people".[50]

A father possesses authority, he is master. He is no less the protector of his offspring. He is wise and is kind. "Our Father" as title of God is no term of the nursery. Father-God, "in him we live and move and have our being".[51] Through him a faithful people belongs to a divine family. "For we are indeed his offspring".[52] But the address of the apostle Paul on Athen's Areopagus is, in the words referred to, a quotation from non-biblical, Greek sources....

---

[50] Isa. lxiv 9.
[51] Acts xvii 28a.
[52] Acts xvii 28b.

MOTHER-GODDESS

Der Gott, der uns in den Himmeln entfloh,
aus der Erde wird er uns wiederkommen

Rainer Maria Rilke

If it should be correct to fix the degree of piety by numbering church-attendance, women are much more pious than men—at least in my country.[1] On many pages of the Old Testament too the influence of women on faith and practice has been very important and it is according to the compilers of the texts in post-exilic times often through women that worship of strange people penetrated into Israelite cult. The Israelites dwelt among the Canaanites, the Hittites, the Amorites, the Perizzites, the Hivites, and the Jebusites; and they took their daughters to themselves for wives, and their own daughters they gave to their sons, and they served their gods [2]—the result of dwelling among the native population of Palestine—forgetting their god Yhwh and serving the Baʿals and the Asherahs, or, better, becoming fused with the inhabitants of the country also concerning worship and faith.

This description in Judges iii is a much more credible record than the picture elsewhere, e.g. in the Book of Joshua, "So Joshua defeated the whole land ... he left none remaining, but utterly destroyed all that breathed, as the Lord, god of Israel, commanded",[3] but the picture of women as point of incidence also might be influenced by the view on women in post-exilic times. Numbers xxv mentions the Israelites becoming integrated with the daughters of Moab. They invited the people to the sacrifices of their gods, and the people ate, and bowed down

---

[1] Compare Alexander Soljenitsyn's acute observation in *L'Archipel du Goulag 1918-1956*, 1974, p. 35: "Durant toutes ces décennies, les femmes fait preuve d'une plus grande fermeté dans la foi".

[2] Judg. iii 5 ff.

[3] Josh. x 40; or similar lines, comp. Ex. xxiii 31 ff, xxxiv 12, 15, Judg. ii 2.

to their gods. King Solomon loved many foreign women [4] and the result is that he introduced foreign cults into Jerusalem and its surroundings. Similarly Ahab in Samaria, erecting an altar for Ba'al and an Asherah, the image of the goddess worshipped by his wife Jezebel.[5]

However, not only were women of the native population and foreigners in the court of the kings condemned by the late Judean theologians because of their promotion of non-Yhwhistic cults. Ma'acah, the mother of Judah's king Asa, daughter of Abishalom, also erected an image of Asherah.[6] Until almost the end of the Judean kingdom worship of Asherah was popular with the women of Jerusalem.[7]

Patai underlines the importance of the Asherah cult. "The Hebrew people, by and large, clung to her for six centuries in spite of the increasing vigor of Yahwist monotheism", he states, o.c. p. 52. He revives the views of Hugo Gressmann [8] and of Julian Morgenstern [9] that the two sacred stones in the Ark originally represented Yhwh and, in all likelihood, his female companion, 'Anat-yahu or Astarte.

Albright, defending a Mosaic monotheism, in the line of the deuteronomistic view on the origin and history of the Israelites, admits irruptions of 'paganism' into Israel and profound in-

---

[4] 1 Kings xi 1.

[5] 1 Kings xvii 32 f.

[6] 1 Kings xv 13. Ma'acah bore, probably, the name of her grandmother. Comp. J. B. Curtis, "East is East....", *JBL* 80, 1961, p. 359 f.

[7] 2 Kings xxiii 7. Several surveys of the female deities of Canaan and their worship have been written. Let it suffice to mention here the archaeological study of Edwin Pilz, "Die weiblichen Gottheiten Kanaans", in *Zeitschrift des deutschen Palestina Vereins* 47, 1924, p. 129-168; W. L. Reed's important thesis, *The Asherah in the Old Testament*, Fort Worth 1949; E. O. James, *The Cult of the Mother-Goddess*, London 1959, chapter III, p. 69 ff, on Israel; R. Patai, *The Hebrew Goddess*, New York 1967; W. F. Albright, *Yahweh and the Gods of Canaan*, London 1968; F. M. Cross, *Canaanite Myth and Hebrew Epic*, Cambridge Mass. 1973.

[8] *Die Lade Jahves*, 1920, p. 64 f.

[9] *Amos Studies* III, *HUCA* 1940, p. 121, n. 98, and *The Ark, the Ephod, and the "Tent of Meeting"*, Cincinnati 1945, p. 95.

fluence from Phoenicia on the literature of later Israel. But Israelite authors, he thinks, were able to utilize it without permitting it seriously to distort their monotheistic approach, o.c. p. 180. In my opinion Th. J. Meek's critique of Albright's view on monotheism [10] is still in force.

The behaviour of almost every king, in Israel but also in Judah, is condemned in the deuteronomistic as well as in the priestly review of history. This review of the history of the people is a serious attempt to explain why Jerusalem and Judah, why David's dynasty and why the temple cult in Jerusalem came to a disastrous end. The 'abominations' for which the Israelites and the Judeans were seduced by their wives, by their kings and queens, by their priests also, are considered to be the cause of the ruin of the two kingdoms. This view is influenced by prophetic oracles from early times, which might have been handed down in certain circles of the people. "Do you not see what they are doing in the cities of Judah and in the streets of Jerusalem?" asks the prophet from Benjamin, Jeremiah.[11] "The children gather wood, the fathers kindle fire, and the women kneed dough, to make cakes for the Queen of heaven". The whole family is engaged, but if a judgment is given, women come first, worshippers of the goddess.

The question can be put: Did the Yhwh cult not satisfy their religious demands? Already in 1908 Max Löhr refuted this assumption of Wellhausen, Smend and others.[12] He sums up the names of women, amongst them a number composed with the name of Israel's God. He points at the name-giving by the mother; the social status of women, indicating some rights and respect. In that connection I mention the obligation of children to honour their family, "honour your father and mother"; [13]

---

[10] *Journal of Biblical Literature* 61, 1942, p. 21-43.
[11] Jer. vii 17 f.
[12] *Die Stellung des Weibes zur Jahwe-Religion und -Kult*, Leipsic 1909.
[13] Ex. xx 12, Deuter. v 16.

David's care for his parents;[14] Rahab's condition that her family should be saved.[15] In a number of cases a woman fulfils the role of a go-between, interceding for the weak party, e.g. the wife of Nabal, Abigail, who kept David from bloodguilt;[16] the woman in Endor, a medium between Saul and Samuel;[17] the woman of Tekoah, interceding for Absalom in Joab's name;[18] the mother of Solomon, Bathsheba, on behalf of her son;[19] Esther; Judith. One is inclined to think of the role of 'Anat in the Ugaritic texts and of the ancient meaning of embassy, *pater patratus*, "the father made father"; and *mater nata ac facta*, mother in a natural sense and also ceremonially dedicated as mother in the Mithraic cult.[20]

During the yearly feast of Yhwh at Shiloh the daughters of the town came out to dance.[21] Elkanah, the Ephraimite, used to go up year by year to worship and to sacrifice to the Lord at Shiloh, together with his family.[22] One of his wives, Hannah, prays and vows a vow at the temple.[23] There were ministering women, with mirrors at the door of the sanctuary, undoubtedly engaged in the cult.[24]

Nevertheless it is stated, "Three times in the year shall all your males see the face of the Lord (or, according to the Masoretic vocalisation, appear before the Lord)".[25] Women, surely joining in the pilgrimages, and also engaged in the

---

[14] 1 Sam. xxii 3.
[15] Josh. iii 13, 18; vi 23.
[16] 1 Sam. xxv.
[17] 1 Sam. xxviii.
[18] 2 Sam. xiv.
[19] 1 Kings i.
[20] See W. B. Kristensen, *Het mysterie van Mithra*, 1946, reprinted in *Symbool en Werkelijkheid*, Arnhem 1954; and *The Meaning of Religion*, The Hague 1960, p. 325 and 366 ff.
[21] Judg. xxi 21, 23.
[22] 1 Sam. i.
[23] 1 Sam. i 9 f.
[24] Ex. xxxviii 8.
[25] Ex. xxiii 17; comp. xxxiv 23.

customs of sacral intercourse at the sanctuaries, are not equal to men in the cultic regulations. They are not called for sacrifice and do not act as a priest.

I have already said that the ruin of the kingdoms was imputed to the putting of the Yhwh cult on a par with the Baʻal cult, and to the worship of Asherah, Anat, Astarte. This evaluation may have been the promoting of the regulations of the cult in post-exilic times as a matter for men only. The idea of a Mother-Goddess in the Yhwhistic cult became unsuitable. It must not be lost sight of that the texts handed down to us, and soon considered to be "holy scripture"—the revelation of the will of God, the starting-point for the religious rules—, were collected, compiled, re-written by *men*. Secondly that almost all description of the past is done by *those who survived*. We are more or less obliged to take into account these facts, and to give special attention to gaps in the tradition, to evident reconstructions, to data which show differences between them. Also to the scarcely visible or even hidden traces of piety. The unity in performance of Israelite piety, suggested by an original monotheism, is a simplification, far from the reality of life.[26]

Botterweck and Ringgren did not insert in their Theological Dictionary of the Old Testament [27] the vocable ʼēm, mother. Jenni-Westermann's less comprehensive but also very instructive Dictionary [28] contains a well composed article on Mother, written by J. Kühlewein. Our subject is very summarily treated in this article. Kühlewein mentions Hosea's conception of the faithless mother, symbolizing Israel.[29] The prophet's figurative language is derived from Canaanite mythology, and is applied to conflict against Israel's disposition to the Canaanite

---

[26] See below. Comp. also my treatment of Gen. ix 8-17 "Quelques remarques sur l'Arc dans la Nuée", in *Questions disputées de l'Ancien Testament*, Louvain 1974, p. 105 f.

[27] *ThWzAT*, Stuttgart 1970 f.

[28] *THAT*, Münich 1971, Vol. I.

[29] Hos. ii 4, 7.

cult with its prostitution, according to this scholar. In Ezekiel xvi we have a reference to the same practice. But nowhere is the term mother, thus Kühlewein, directly characterizing Yhwh. Yhwh is in the Old Testament conception a male deity. Only once, in post-exilic times, Yhwh's activity is compared with motherly conduct, "As one whom his mother comforts, so will I comfort you",[30] a strophe which can be compared with

> "Can a woman—'*ishshāh* is used here—forget her suckling child, that she should have no compassion on the son of her womb? Even these may forget, yet I will not forget you".[31]

So far Kühlewein.

A mother-goddess in Israelite and Judean piety is a rare phenomenon indeed. However, something more than is stated by Kühlewein can be observed about the mother-title and about feminine aspects of the God of Israel.

Deborah is called "a mother in Israel". She is the leading character of the song in Judges v, and in the narrative about a battle against king Jabin's general Sisera, chapter iv, she is named "a prophetess, judging Israel". This means she possesses authority. There is nothing of a motherly character in the picture of Deborah. In the song she is the bellicose leader of the united tribes. Her conduct reminds one of the goddess, pictured in several texts from Mesopotamia and Syria.[32] In Hammurabi's Code, in the epilogue, is Inanna's epithet "the Lady of the Battle". Esarhaddon (680-669) states: "Ishtar, the Lady of the Battle, who likes me (to be) her highpriest, stood at my side breaking bows, scattering their orderly battle array".[33] Nabonidus says about her, "without whom neither hostilities nor

---

[30] Isa. lxvi 13.
[31] Isa. xlix 15.
[32] Cf. A. S. Kapelrud, *Anat, the violent goddess*, Oslo 1969; P. D. Miller, *The divine warrior in early Israel*, Cambridge Mass. 1973; F. M. Cross, *Canaanite Myth and Hebrew Epic, o.c.*
[33] Translation of A. Leo Oppenheim, *ANET*², *o.c.* p. 289.

reconciliation can occur in the country and no battle can be fought".³⁴ In a detailed article W. Herrmann concludes about Astarte,³⁵ "Despite the accepted opinion of her as a goddess of fecundity and sexual love she has, on the contrary, a pugnacious character, interferes in battles herself and is reputed to be the protector of justice and order among gods and men." The Ugaritic goddess ʿAnat too is a "violent goddess", the title of A. S. Kapelrud's monograph,³⁶ a warrior. However, it remains open to discussion whether a bellicose character is in contrast with being a goddess of fertility and sexual love.

ʿAnat-yahu is a Judean goddess, mentioned in the Aramaic papyri from Elephantine, Egypt, 5th century B.C. She is Yhwh's consort. Her cult in the Judean community can hardly have been an innovation.³⁷

Deborah possesses authority, and as a Lady of the Battle she is active. As a mother she gives the just decision from which life or death depends. To have authority will be the precise meaning of the root *shāphat*.³⁸ The rabbinic phrase, *yesh ʾēm lĕmiqrāʾ*, there is a mother for the reading, means too there is authority for the reading.³⁹

Heinrich Margulies published recently a remarkable study, "Das Rätsel der Biene".⁴⁰ Proceeding from Samson's riddle,

"Out of the eater came something to eat
out of the strong came something sweet" ⁴¹

he dealt with Deborah = honey, picturing her as a goddess, the Bee, from Aegean origin, worshipped as a mother of all living.

---

³⁴ *Supplements to ANAT*, p. 526.
³⁵ In *Mitteilungen des Instituts für Orientforschung* XV, Berlin 1969, p. 6-52.
³⁶ Kapelrud, *o.c.*
³⁷ Thus rightly James, *o.c.* p. 80.
³⁸ See M. S. Rozenberg's thesis, Pennsylvania 1963, *The Stem ʿšpṭ*: an investigation of Biblical and Extra-Biblical sources.
³⁹ See my "The Counsellor", *a.c.* p. 58 ff, where more can be found on the term 'mother' in Old Testament and Rabbinic literature.
⁴⁰ In *VT* XXIV, 1974, p. 56-76, inventive and well documented.
⁴¹ Judg. xiv 14.

Mother of all living, of all who live—it is Eve's epithet in Genesis iii 20. "Adam called his wife Eve because she was the mother of all living". This verse is without connection with its context. It may preserve a line from an ancient myth. After the story of the building of a woman from one of *hā-'ādām*'s ribs, *hā-'ādām* said,

> "This at last is bone of my bones
> and flesh of my flesh;
> she shall be called *'ishshāh*—woman—
> because she was taken out of *'îsh*—man—."[42]

The term *'îsh* does not occur in the creation story. Man is called *hā-'ādām*, and one would expect the name for *hā-'ādām*'s partner to be *hā-'ădāmāh*. The use of *'îsh* and in connection with it of *'ishshāh* in verse 23 seems to be caused by the sequence, verse 24,

> "Therefore a man—*'îsh*—leaves his father and his mother and cleaves to his wife—*'ishshāh*—".

This must be a secondary text, there was no mention of a family in the story. Margulies assumes a purposely made change to avoid the conception that *hā-'ădāmāh*, the earth, is *hā-'ādām*'s mother. I think this is a second indication that there once existed another myth, wherein the woman is the earth. Eve, in Hebrew *ḥawwāh*, might mean "life". The name is used only twice in the transmitted text, in chapter iii 20, and in chapter iv 1; in the latter even superfluous.

The earth is mother of all living. Even *hā-'ādām* is token from her, "formed of dust from *hā-'ădāmāh*".[43] A single trace of this ancient piety has been preserved in the Book of Job,

> "Naked I came from my mother's womb,
> and naked shall I return there—*shámmāh*—".[44]

---

[42] Gen. ii 23.
[43] Gen. ii 7.
[44] Job i 21. See S. Terrien, *Job*, commentaire, Neuchâtel 1963, p. 57.

The last word, "there", thither, is omitted in the Syriac translation, and also in several modern translations, but I think wrongly. The Septuagint reads ἐκεῖ; the Vulgate *illuc*; and the Targum has an explanatory rendering, *lĕbêt qĕbûrtāʾ*, in the sepulchre. We have to go as far as ben Sira to read again,[45]

"Much labour was created for every man
and a heavy yoke is upon the sons of Adam
from the day they come forth from their mother's womb
till the day they return to the mother of all".
ἕως ἡμέρας ἐπιτροφῆς εἰς μητέρα πάντων.

Mother of all living.

The serpent in the story of Genesis iii has preserved some features of the divine character of the beast. It is distinguished by supernatural wisdom. Compare too the wilderness story about the fiercy Serpent [46] and its veneration at sanctuaries of Israel's God.[47] Albright has given a good characterization of a figurine with two serpents in her hand: "the goddess of life and wisdom".[48]

I assume that the version handed down to us in Genesis ii and iii is a revision, or a substitute of an ancient myth. Mother-Goddess is a conception that must have been felt too much related to the earth, the country, no longer Judean property, too clear a reminiscence of the cult practiced in Jerusalem during the kingdom, a cult in post-exilic times considered to be apostasy and the cause of the ruin. If I am right in this assumption the lack of any clear allusion to the second and third chapter of Genesis in the writings of the Old Testament is no longer a problem. They who have made the revision are in their theological views not far from some passages in the prophetic

---

[45] ben Sira xl 1. A still later witness in 4 Macc. xv 16, 29.
[46] Numb. xxi 4-9.
[47] 1 Kings i 9; 2 Kings xviii 4. Next to the young bull (inscription from Samaria *ʿglyw*; 1 Kings xii 28; Ex. xxxii) the serpent is an attribute of Yhwh.
[48] *AJSL&L* 36, p. 258 ff, 1920.

books of pre-exilic origin, criticizing the cult in Jerusalem and other places.

The Lord's love for the people is like a mother's love and care. The picture of Yhwh, the Lord, as Israel's mother in Numbers xi is remarkably stringent. Moses complains about the unbearable burden which the people are to him. He is, after all, not the mother of the people and is, therefore, not obliged to fulfill maternal duties towards them.

> "Did I conceive—the root *hārāh* is used—all this people? Did I bring them forth?—the root *yālad* is used—that thou should say to me: 'Carry them in your bosom, as a beloved little mother carries the suckling child' ".[49]

The idea of motherhood is expressed here very clearly. Divine motherhood must have been well known in ancient Israel and Judah. The post-exilic compiler of the ancient material could not abolish every trace of this ancient piety.

The idea of motherhood in Hebrew piety is also preserved in comparisons with the world of birds, a conception well known in Egyptian sources. "In the shadow of thy wings I will take refuge" is a frequently used figurative language.[50] The origin of some conceptions in Deuteronomy xxxii may point to the same world.

> "Like an eagle (or, vulture) that stirs up its nest
> that flutters over its young
> spreading out its wings, catching them,
> bearing them on its pinions, ...
> The Lord alone did lead him . . . .".[51]

Hempel [52] thinks that comparisons with the birds were not at

---

[49] Numb. xi 12. "a beloved little mother", read *hā᾿immôn*, cf. Prov. viii 30, see above p. 5; the reading *hā᾿ōmēn* is usually rendered with "a nurse".

[50] Pss lvii 2; lx 5; lxiii 8; xci 4; Ruth ii 12.

[51] Deuter. xxxii 11 f.

[52] J. Hempel, *Gott und Mensch im Alten Testament*, sec. ed., Stuttgart 1936, p. 184.

home in the Yhwhistic religion because of their origin in the cult of female deities. However, this opinion stands or falls by the correctness of the traditional Judeo-Christian view on Israel's God as only a male deity.

Friedrich Haeussermann has used psychological ideas to explain the motherhood phase of religion as a more "primitive" one than the fatherhood phase.[53] The Canaanite religion should be the motherhood phase, with sentiments and sensuality, with prayers for protection, help and comfort. The Yhwh religion should be the fatherhood phase, believing in a powerful deity, with fear, fright and admiration. The prophets have emphasized the idea of trust in the Father-God, whose relation with the people is no longer through birth but by adoption.

It is, in my opinion, a credit that Haeussermann acknowledges that other religions than the Israelite religion also considered their gods not a mere natural divine power. His description of divine motherhood, however, has overlooked the fighting character of several goddesses. He is right in observing that in times of disaster the Lord appears to be, in more than ethical sense, a father ánd a mother for his believers.

Application of the term "primitive" to the motherhood phase of religion is a weak point in Haeussermann's study. Kristensen has warned often against an easy use of terms as "primitive" and "development" in historical research of ancient religions. Guthrie also rejects a facile use of such terms. Dealing with the phenomenon "empty thrones" he says, "Now chronologically it is true that empty thrones came before sculptured gods, and that orgiastic rites like those of Dionysos or the Great Mother are older than the Olympian religion of Homer. If that is all that we mean, we may call them more primitive, but it does not follow that there was progress from one to the other. That depends on what our criterion of progress is. If it is the growth

---

[53] *Wortempfang und Symbol in den alttestamentlichen Prophetie*, Eine Untersuchung zur Psychologie der prophetischen Erlebnissen, *BZAW* 58, 1932.

of spiritual insight, there is much to be said for the view that the man who carves a stone seat and leaves it for the God to occupy when he will, asking only to see him with the eye of the imagination, is at a higher stage of religious development than the man who demands to see the God in physical form, carved by the hand of a Pheidias. Similarly the Dionysiac idea of communion and identification with the God, or the belief of the worshipper of the Mother-Goddess that he could be adopted into the family of his deity, together with the other mystical forms of religion practised from time immemorial in Aegean lands, contained, despite their crudeness, possibilities of spiritual development which were lacking to the religion of Homer".[54]

The conception of motherhood in the Biblical texts may be scarcely professed, yet there exist, in my opinion, enough indications that ancient Israel and Judah have worshipped motherly aspects of their God.

The Gospels bear witness to the continuity of this form of ancient piety,

> "O Jerusalem, Jerusalem, killing the prophets and stoning who are sent to you:
> How often would I have gathered your children together as a hen gathers her brood under her wings,
> and you would not." [55]

---

[54] W. B. Kristensen, *Primitieve Wijsheid* (1952) in *Symbool en Werkelijkheid*, o.c.; *The meaning of Religion*, o.c. p. 13 and *passim*; W. K. C. Guthrie, *The Greek and their Gods*, o.c. p. 34.

[55] Matth. xxiii 37, cf. Luke xiii 34.

GOD: FATHER AND MOTHER

The true order and origin of our existence is from an Eternal Parentage

John H. Morgan *

When the prophet Elijah cast his mantle upon Elisha,[1] who was ploughing his field, Elisha left the oxen, and ran after Elijah. He said to him: "Let me kiss my father and my mother, and then I will follow you". Elijah's answer to this request is called "enigmatic" in the recent commentary of John Gray.[2] Fohrer, in his monograph on Elijah,[3] thinks the answer a rebuke to Elisha, who had not realized the full significance of the prophetic call. Elijah's answer was,

"Go back, for what have I made you?"

Gray's paraphrase is slightly different: "Go, but (remember) what I have done to you". The New English Bible reads, "Go back, what have I done to prevent you?" Those renderings, I think, do not fit into the context. Elijah's casting the prophet's mantle, symbol of his dignity, upon Elisha means a divine call which introduces the anointment to be a prophet of the Lord in Elijah's place. Elisha has to leave his family, his kinship group, to become a man of God, a man with "a new heart", i.e. a man guided by a new will. His request to kiss his father and his mother, to finish his life as a son of the family in order to enter into a new life, is allowed. His farewell to his family is the consequence of his vocation. The new Oxford Annotated Bible [4]

---

* Motto from "Eternal Father-Eternal Mother in Shaker Theology", Inward Light, Spring 1973; quoted in Ermine Huntress Lantero, *Feminine Aspects of Divinity, o.c.*

[1] 1 Kings xix 19 ff.
[2] *I & II Kings*, sec. ed., London 1970.
[3] G. Fohrer, *Elia*, sec. ed., Zürich 1968.
[4] Revised Standard Version, ed. by H. G. May and B. H. Metzger, 1973.

explains the last part of Elijah's answer rightly, saying, ".... for I have done something very important to you".

Elisha slaughtered the oxen, burnt the wooden yoke to cook the flesh and had a farewell dinner with his folk—the term used, '*am*, can include the whole family—. "Then he arose", says verse 21 end, "and went after Elijah, and ministered him".

Genesis ii 24 expresses a similar definite farewell, the transition into a new position and new life,

> "Therefore a man leaves his father and his mother and cleaves to his wife, and they become one flesh".

Following Jesus means a same definite parting from one's own relations, according to the Gospels. In Mark iii 31-35 we read,

> "And his—Jesus'—mother and brothers came; and standing outside they sent to him and called him. And a crowd was sitting about him; and they said to him: 'Your mother and your brothers are outside, asking for you'. And he replied, 'Who are my mother and my brothers?' And looking around on those who sat about him, he said, 'Here are my mother and my brothers. Whoever does the will of God is my brother, and sister, and mother' ".

Compare also Jesus' word, "He who loves father or mother more than me is not worthy of me....", Matthew x 37.

Father and mother are considered to be a unity. They are the centre of a family. Leaving them means to transit into a new form of life,—or to be lost.

In the epilogue to the Code of Hammurabi the God Enlil and his consort Ninlil are complements to each other. The same can be said about El and Asherah in the Ugaritic texts. Several Egyptian Gods are named at the same time father and mother.[5]

---

[5] References to Egyptian texts are from K. Sethe, *Urgeschichte und älteste Religion der Aegypter*, Leipsic 1930; H. Kees, *Der Götterglaube im alten Aegypten*, Leipsic 1941; J. Zandee, *De hymnen aan Amon van Papyrus Leiden I 350*, Leiden 1947; S. Sauneron, *Les Fêtes Religieuses d'Esna*, Cairo 1962. I desire to acknowledge my general indebtness to these writers.

Amun, Ptah, Osiris, the primordial Gods are fathers and mothers, origin of life, and this twofold unity is before the creation potentially present in Nûn. The sun-god is called "the excellent mother of gods and men". Amun is called "father of the fathers, mother of the mothers", a title used since the 19th dynasty. Amun is the origin of the male and the female principle. Containing the paternal and maternal principle in himself, Amun is both father and mother of all the generations of gods, following after him. In hymns from the temple of Khnum, the creator, we read the same title, "Father of the fathers, mother of the mothers". ".... the mistress of the milk .... mother of the egg, who makes the unborn children breathe in the pregnant woman".[6]

Next to these Egyptian texts I refer to a Hittite prayer from *circa* 1430 B.C., addressing the sun-goddess of Ariana,

".... of every country you are father and mother".[7]

Father and mother as title of a goddess is the clearest indication that we should not limit the term "father-mother" to the sexual relation of male and female divine beings or men. Something more is expressed in the religious language of those ancient believers. Father, mother, father and mother are terms expressing, next to creative power, protection, maintenance of life, authority—all in all the divine form of what is daily experience in family life.

According to a Phoenician inscription from Sidon,[8] a priestess of Astarte is named *'ēm 'astart*, mother (is) Astarte. The

---

[6] Sauneron, *o.c.* p. 66; 206; 226 f ".... le père des pères, la mère des mères .... maîtresse du lait .... mère de l'oeuf, qui fait respirer la gorge angoissé des enfants, dans le ventre de la femme enceinte ....". I am indebted to Dr B. Stricker for these quotations.

[7] Translation of M. Vieyra in *Les religions du proche-orient*, Paris 1970, p. 557, "Toi, ô déesse solaire d'Arinna .... De chaque pays tu es le père et la mère ....".

[8] *KAI* No. 14; Rosenthal in *ANET*², p. 226, *Suppl. to ANET*, p. 662.

goddess Ishtar is addressed as a lioness and at the same time as a lion, in her aspect as goddess of valour and of war. She is called "my God and my Goddess".[9]

But enough examples of the double term "father and mother". The Gods who are thus addressed are believed to help in periods of danger, in cases of illness, pains of child-birth, of war, famine, flood or drought. A special sexual qualification does not stand in the foreground.

Kurt Leese published a small book, *Die Mutter als religiöses Symbol*,[10] in which is rightly said, "das Muttersymbol steckt im Vatersymbol", the symbol "mother" is involved in the symbol "father". Leese's observation refers to New Testament texts but we can pursue it also to several Od Testament passages. In the second part of the Book of Isaiah a preacher says to "the remnant of Israel's house", the Judean exiles in Babylonia,

> "who have been borne by me from the belly, carried from the womb, and until your old age I am he, and to gray hairs am I carrying you. Since I have made, I will both bear, carry and save".[11]

Such a divine carrier is a real saviour. "In his love and in his pity he redeemed them; he lifted them up and carried them all the days of old".[12]

To carry small children is a motherly task. We find the same figurative language in Exodus xix, "You have seen what I did to the Egyptians, and how I bore you on eagle's wings and brought you to myself", verse 4.

---

[9] *ANET*², p. 383 ff. The titles "king" and "queen" are used similar to "father" and "mother", comp. "Narru, king of the gods, who created mankind", parallel to "the goddess Mami, the queen who fashioned them". *Suppl. to ANET*, p. 601 ff.
[10] Tübingen 1934.
[11] Isa. xlvi 3 f. See my *Second-Isaiah's Message*, Leiden 1956, p. 20, 50.
[12] Isa. lxiii 9b.

In the "Song of Moses", Deuteronomy xxxii, the conception of Yhwh as mother and father is preserved,[13]

"You were unmindful of the Rock that bore you
and you forgot the God who gave you birth".

The reading *yĕlādĕkā*, "that bore you", qal, is unequivocal and its rendering cannot be mistaken. The rendering "that begot you", reading a hiph'il, is against the text transmitted to us, or assuming a meaning of the qal that this form is not carrying.[14]

With great pastoral care post-exilic writers point to the pre-history of the people now they, the remnant coming back from exile, are in a similar situation. No king, no state, no possession of the country, but a small community wherein the priests took over the authority of the king and speak of "a kingdom of priests" and "a holy people", living amidst pagans—according to their opinion—and under foreign domination.

It is instructive to observe that the religious rules and observances, sabbath, passover, circumcision—the backbone of Judean post-exilic piety—all have been fixed, projected in pre-historic times. The great acts of the Lord on behalf of the people, the redemption from slavery, the promise of a land and the rules for living in the promised land, temple and kingship and their divine laws—everything was to have been prepared and fixed before the real history of Israel and Judah began in Palestine.[15] The whole time that the kingdoms existed is—

---

[13] verse 18. Comp. the apostle Paul: "For I became your father..." 1 Cor. iv 15b, and "My little children, with whom I am again in travail..." Gal. iv 19a.

[14] I owe this passage to Phyllis Trible and W. L. Holladay, Andover Newton Theological School. Professor Trible's paper "Depatriarchalizing in Biblical Interpretation", *Journal of the American Academy of Religion* 41, 1, 1973, p. 30 ff, which she kindly presented to me, contains original ideas on Genesis ii-iii and the Song of Songs, cognated to the subject of these lectures.

[15] I think, however, that "Heilsvorgeschichte", pre-history of salvation, will be a less attractive term than the popular but unhistorical slogan "Heilsgeschichte"....

according to their opinion—a dark period full of abominations. With a simple story of the election of one family, the story of Abraham, Isaac and Jacob, and a narrative full of miracles, from Egypt to Palestine, a liturgy for worship and every day life was constructed. This became a "stabilized piety", established faith, a guarantee for uniformity and "apartheid", separation; a real home, a family, kinship group, in its fusion of blood-relationship and religious rules a strong, closed corporation. Perhaps it was the only way for the remnant to recover their identity and to cherish expectations after the ruin of David's dynasty, the exile and the deceptions after the return to Palestine. But as a "stabilized" piety it became also an impediment, hampering any belief in new and unexpected acts of God.

The idea of the Lord married to the country, or to the city, is found in the second part of the Book of Isaiah.[16] "Thus says the Lord: 'Where then is the bill of divorce of your mother whom I sent away? And who is my creditor to whom I have sold you?—words alluding to the legal rights of a husband to divorce himself from his wife, and of a father to sell his children. The text continues, 'Behold, for your iniquities were you sold, and for your rebellions was your mother sent away'". The Lord is in this picture husband and father. The exile, however, is no indication that he practised his fatherly rights because of his own difficulties. The desolation of Judah and the exile of its inhabitants are a punishment for the rebellions and iniquities of the Judean people. Second-Isaiah continues with the idea of the desolate wife and the sold children: exiled Judah is not definitively divorced, there exists no bill of divorce. And as a father the Lord possesses legal rights to redeem, acting as kinsman, *gô'ēl*, redeemer of his children.

The symbol of the Lord's marriage with the people was already used in the 8th century B.C. by the prophet Hosea.[17]

---
[16] Isa. l 1.
[17] Hos. i-iii.

Jeremiah's tender figurative language is a striking example of the same picture. He makes the Lord say, [18]

> "I remember [19] the devotion of your youth,
> your love as a bride,
> how you followed me in the wilderness
> in a land not sown....".[20]

I assumed the possibility that Wisdom in Proverbs viii is designed as the Lord's inspiring consort.[21] From her love-play the world was born. Further on I dealt with traces of the conception of the Mother of all living in the texts handed down to us. In an archaeological study of the religious past in Ancient Palestine [22] W. C. Graham and H. G. May have given much attention to a bronze figurine of the Mother-Goddess found in Gezer. They refer to more examples of horned goddesses and think that the motivation for this representation of the earth-mother was originally the desire to draw the nomadic-pastoral elements of the population—the fertility of the flock—into the cultic pattern of the more native population—with the serpent mother-goddess figurines—the fertility of the field. There must have been a rather close connection between the Yhwh cult and the Astarte cult. God and the Goddess seem to have stood side by side in Mizpah, in the 9th century B.C.

Yhwh and his Consort as a phenomenon of the Yhwhistic cult one does not find in the many books on "the" theology of the Old Testament written since 1936. I suppose that almost all theologians feel themselves too much bound by the "stabilized piety" of the post-exilic writers.

---

[18] Jer. ii 2.
[19] "remember", the root *zkr* is used here, which can be paraphrased by "I make present, I make vivid to me", see my *Gedenken und Gedächtniss in der Welt des Alten Testaments*, Stuttgart 1962.
[20] Comp. further Jer. iii 4, 19, quoted above, p. 15.
[21] In the first lecture, see above p. 4 f.
[22] *Culture and Conscience*, Chicago 1936, p. 162.

However, it must be admitted that the instances produced so far are not a conclusive evidence of a close relation between the Yhwh cult and the Astarte cult. Its probability might gain in strength by a new explanation of one of the most discussed verses of the Old Testament, Genesis i 26. In the usual rendering we find, "Then God said, Let us make man in our image, after our likeness . . . .".

"And God said" occurs several times in Genesis i. The expression meant the decision and command of God. God's decision and command were recognized by the believer in the wind which brought rain and thus fertility, in the storm from the wilderness which resulted in dryness and destruction. The prophetic formula, "Thus says the Lord", also has this background. The prophet points to the event which he expects, or which, according to him, already exists or has taken place, all as the decision and command of Israel's God. God's decision and command also make heaven and earth. Second-Isaiah is able to place the myth of creation side by side with the edict of Cyrus as a new creation. His God made heaven and earth and now creates a new city, Jerusalem, from the chaos which the fall of the kingdom has brought with it.[23]

In Genesis i verses 3, 6, 9, 11, 14, 20, 24 God is evidently commanding his servants, like a king in his court. Creation by a magic word, by speech only, is documented very early on in Babylonia and Egypt. Psalm xxxiii seems to point in such a direction: "For he spoke and it came to be". "By the word of the Lord the heavens were made, and all their host by the breath of his mouth", verses 9a and 6. But in the same song is said: "He commanded, and it stood forth", verse 9b; and in speaking of the Lord's work, "he gathered the waters of the sea as in a bottle, he put the deeps in storehouses", verse 7. Moreover, in Genesis i is added to "And God said": "And God saw that it

---

[23] Comp. a.o. F. Holmgren's recently published valuable study *With Wings as Eagles, Isaiah 40/55*, Chappaqua N.Y. 1973.

was good", verses 10, 12, 18, 25, 31. After a creative magic word it is unnecessary to state, "and God saw that it was good". But after a command a sentence can be added wherein is said that God approved the work done by his servants at his command. My tentative rendering is therefore: "And God approved it."

But whom is God commanding in verse 26? Since early times—ancient versions, the rabbinic explanations—an answer to this question is found by rendering what God is saying as a cohortative, "Let us make. ...", ποιήσωμεν, *faciamus*; rabbi Ammi said, He took counsel with his own heart. W. H. Schmidt, who wrote a very instructive monograph on the creation story,[24] assumes a *pluralis deliberationis*, a deliberation in a soliloquy of God.[25] However, the idea of deliberation is usually expressed in Hebrew by (literally) saying in the heart, see a.o. Genesis viii 21: "the Lord said in his heart". A more serious objection against the assumption of a soliloquy of God seems to be the dissimilarity in the meaning of the used formula, seven times a command and in our verse a difference. G. W. Ahlström rejects the idea of soliloquizing too.[26] God is, according to him, addressing the assembly of Gods. In this assembly were to be found male and female deities. But he too assumes a deliberation and abandons the idea of command in our verse.

The Hebrew text is not necessarily cohortative and can be rendered by, "We shall make". The plural is continued in the sequence, "We shall make people (*'ādām*) in the form of *our* image, looking like *us*". The result of the making is also a plural: "God blessed *them*", verse 28.

All these reasons point at a God and a Goddess as subject of "We shall make people". God, pictured as a king with a court,

---

[24] *Die Schöpfungsgeschichte*, sec. ed., Neukirchen-Vluyn 1967.
[25] Schmidt is followed by Cl. Westermann, *Genesis*, Biblischer Kommentar, Neukirchen-Vluyn, in process of being published.
[26] *Aspects of Syncretism in Israelite Religion*, Lund 1963, p. 50.

making heaven and earth through creative royal strength, makes man. The ancient believer recognised man's fertility and power as a gift of his God who himself is male and female. Only if man is conscious of holiness in his being man and woman he might be able to understand that a conception of God: Father and Mother, guarantee of life and existence, is no blasphemy but expression of true faith.

J. Hempel, who has assumed a *Vorlage* of the priestly source wherein a god and a goddess occurred whose image man receives,[27] rightly observed that a priestly source cannot be the origin of this conception. I think it is still possible to distinguish in the text handed down to us in the first chapter of Genesis two ancient creation myths, and next to them an explanatory addition composed by priestly writers. I am working on the idea of Stade and Schwally who independently of each other in the beginning of our century suggested to distinguish between God making the world and God creating by his word.[28] I assume two ancient myths in Genesis i, one wherein God as a divine handicraftsman, like the potter in prophetical sayings, fashioned heaven and earth, and a second myth wherein God as a king, like Yhwh-King in several psalms, made heaven and earth. God as a king was acting with court and consort.

These myths must have been known and favourite until the times of the priestly writers. These writers made, in my opinion, a compilation of the myths and added to the composition their own ideas about the identity of the community which they tried to guide through the uncertain times after the exile. Their additions—in my translation which is added to this lecture in

---

[27] "Gott, Mensch und Tier im Alten Testament mit besonderer Berücksichtigung von Gen. 1-3", *Zeitschrift für systemathische Theologie* XI 2, 1931; reprinted in *Apoxysmata, BZAW* 81, 1961.

[28] B. Stade, *Biblische Theologie des Alten Testament* I, Tübingen 1905; F. Schwally, "Die biblischen Schöpfungsberichte", *Archiv für Religions-Wissenschaft* 9, 1906, p. 159 ff.

italics—are a systematization, the sabbath once in seven days; the generic description; the order to become numerous; the dominion by man over nature; regulations about food. Systematization can be called an attempt to master a complicated situation. It can be compared with canonization. Canons are adopted under political pressure.[29] Dogma's also are formulated in times of crisis, in defence against enmity and hostility, and for protection against temptations.

We should not stress the idea of sexuality when we read in an ancient Israelite creation myth of God being father and mother of man. Sexuality is in our days set loose from piety and also from family life. It is not an imaginary danger that the mysterious character is lost and humanity is affected. New understanding of God's "Eternal Parentage" could be a remedy.

---

[29] Comp. E. C. Colwell, *The Study of the Bible*, Chicago 1937; 7th ed. 1953.

GENESIS I 1 - II 4a

Two creation myths and priestly additions [1]

(i 1) *As heading:* GOD FASHIONED HEAVEN AND EARTH. (2) AS FOR THE EARTH, IT WAS SODDEN WASTELAND, DARKNESS OVER THE DEEP AND HURRICANE WHIRLING OVER THE WATERS. (3) And God said: Let there be light! *And there came light.* (4) And God approved the light. GOD NOW SEPARATED LIGHT AND DARKNESS. (5) *And God called the light day and the darkness he called night. And it became evening and it became morning: the first day.* (6) And God said: Let there be a firmament in the waters and let the waters be separated! (7) AND GOD MADE THE FIRMAMENT AND THE WATERS HE SEPARATED INTO WATERS FROM UNDERNEATH THE FIRMAMENT AND WATERS FROM ABOVE THE FIRMAMENT. *And it happened in this way.* (8) *And God called the firmament heaven. And it became evening and it became morning, the second day.* (9) And God said: Let the waters be collected in one place so that the dry part can be laid bare. *And it happened in this way.* (10) *And God called the dryness earth and the piled-up waters he called sea.* And God approved it. (11) And God said: Let the earth make young verdure sprout, seed producing herbs, fruit trees which produce fruit *according to their sort which contain their seed on the earth. And it happened in this way.* (12) *The earth now brought forth young verdure, seed producing herbs according to their sort, and fruit trees which contain the seed of their sort.* And God approved it. (13) *And it became evening and it became morning: the third day.* (14) And God said: Let there be lights on the firmament of the heaven! *in*

---

[1] This translation and exposition is no more than an attempt to explain the divergency in style and in conception of this chapter. There exists, in my opinion, no reason to suppose a priestly source. The priestly part, here in italics, is additional and probably of more than one hand. The myth wherein God is pictured as a handicraftman, printed with small capitals, seems to be completely preserved in the compilation, the second one with God as king is incomplete.

order to keep the day and the night apart. They will then indicate the fixed seasons, the days and the years. (15) They will be the lights on the firmament of heaven enlightening the earth. And it happened in this way. (16) AND GOD MADE THE TWO GREAT LIGHTS the great light ruling over the day and the small light ruling over the night AND THE STARS. (17) AND GOD PLACED THEM ON THE FIRMAMENT OF THE HEAVEN. Enlightening the earth (18) and ruling over day and night, keeping too light and darkness apart. And God approved it. (19) And it became evening and it became morning: the fourth day. (20) And God said: The waters must teem with a mass of animals, and birds must fly over the earth and at the firmament of the heaven. (21) THEN GOD FASHIONED THE GREAT SEA-MONSTERS AND EVERYTHING WHICH CREEPS wherefrom the waters swarm, according to their sort AND ALL FLYING BIRDS. According to their sort. And God approved it. (22) And God blessed them. Saying: Be fruitful and multiply and make the water and the seas full, let the birds be numerous on earth. (23) And it became evening and it became morning: the fifth day. (24) And God said: Let the earth produce creatures according to their sort, domesticated animals, creeping animals and wild animals according to their sort. And it happened in this way. (25) FURTHER GOD MADE THE WILD ANIMALS, according to their sort, THE DOMESTICATED ANIMALS according to their sort, AND ALL THE CREEPING ANIMALS ON THE SOIL. According to their sort. And God approved it. (26) And God said: We shall make people in the form of our image, looking like us so that they will rule over the fishes of the sea and over the birds of the heaven and over the domesticated animals and over the wild animals and over the creeping beasts on earth. (27) THEN GOD FASHIONED MAN. IN THE SHAPE OF HIS IMAGE, IN THE SHAPE OF A DIVINE IMAGE HE FASHIONED HIM. Male and female he fashioned them. (28) And God blessed them. And God said to them: Be fruitful and become numerous and fill the earth and subject it, and rule over the fishes of the sea, over the birds of the heaven and over all the beasts which creep on the earth. (29) And God said: I, behold, I give you all the seed bearing herbs that are on the *surface of the whole earth and every fruit tree with seed bearing fruit. They will be your food.* (30) *And every wild animal and all the birds of heaven and everything that creeps on the earth in which there is life, all the green verdure for food. And it happened in this way.* (31) And God mightly approved everything he had made. *And it became evening and it became morning: the sixth day.*

(ii 1) Then the heaven and the earth and all their hosts were completed. (2) *And on the seventh day God completed his work which he was doing and he entirely stopped his work that he was doing on the seventh day.* (3) *And God blessed the seventh day and consecrated it, for on it he stopped all the work which God actively had fashioned.* (4a) *This is the story of the heaven and the earth, when they were fashioned.*

EPILOGUE

Family is named a condition for life. It was no matter of surprise to find epithets of God borrowed from the relationship in the kinship group. For God is for his believers the utmost condition for life.

Father and Mother as titles of God are less frequent than we should suppose, however. Non-literal use of the terms outside and within Israel points towards outstanding people representing God's fatherhood: kings, stewards, Levites, prophets, wise men and women, counsellors; and towards divine fatherhood concerning countries and cities and their inhabitants.

Striking features are:

a) divine two-fold unity worshipped as the origin of life and as the only salvation in times of disaster;
b) no emphasis laid on begetting or sexuality;
c) a bellicose character of a female deity is no contrast to her fertility character;
d) addressed as Father and Mother God is giving fertility, and also justice, order, wisdom—divine likeness as a blessing and commission;
e) a prophetic stress on vocation to leave one's family relation, to transit into a new, spiritual relation.

After the fall of the Davidic dynasty and in the post-exilic centuries life and worship of the remnant have been fixed upon an evaluation of the history of the people and a reconstruction of their origin in prehistoric times. Historical data and ancient myths and legends are mixed up with experiences and expectations of post-exilic times in the version of the biblical texts handed down to us. God's Fatherhood is shaped as the Lord's election of Abraham and his seed. God's Motherhood is pressed back. However, several traces of ancient piety became clear, directly and indirectly.

In my introductory remarks I stated that Fatherhood and Motherhood as divine qualities are no more than one aspect of Israelite and Judean piety and I wish to repeat this. I have tried to limit myself to the subject but I could not avoid some aspects of larger scope, nor some problems of our own spiritual situation. I hope that it became clear that the Bible, dissociated from the traditional theory: "Holy Scripture", preserves more aspects than are deemed fit in the religion of Israel and that some of them are giving a new vision.

Praying to God, "Our Father who art in heaven" and forgetting the Mother of all living, is inadequate. Praying to "Our Mother who art in earth" and forgetting the fatherly authority, is likewise inadequate. Due to what became visible of divine Fatherhood and Motherhood in ancient Israelite and Judean piety we ought, I think, to pray to God's totality, respectfully desiring to belong to his family. The most adequate prayer will be a silent prayer for *when we are silent we are one, when we speak we are two.*

INDEX

a) BIBLICAL AND OTHER REFERENCES

Genesis

i 1-ii 4a   23, 45 ff, 49 ff
i 3, 6, 9, 11, 14, 20, 24   45
i 10, 12, 18, 25, 31   45 f
i 26   45 ff
i 28   46
ii-iii   34, 42
ii 7   33
ii 23   33
ii 24   33, 39
iii   34
iii 20   33
iv 1   33
iv 20-22   18
viii 21   46
ix 8-17   30
xxiii 4   8
xli 16   19
xli 39 ff   19
xlv 8   19

Exodus

iv 22b, 23   23
x 7 ff   7
xix 4   41
xx 12   28
xxiii 17   29
xxiii 31 ff   26
xxxii   34
xxxiv 12, 15   26
xxxiv 23   29
xxxviii 8   29

Leviticus

xxvii 1 ff   6 f

Numbers

xi 12   35
xxi 4-9   34

Deuteronomy

v 16   28
viii 5   20
x 18   12
xxxii 6   15, 24 f
xxxii 11 f   35
xxxii 18   42
xxxiii 9   11 f, 18

Joshua

iii 13, 18   29
vi 23   29
x 40   26

Judges

ii 2   26
iii 5 ff   26
iv, v   31 f
xiv 14   32
xvii, xviii   18 f
xvii 7, 10 f   18
xviii 19   18 f
xxi 21, 23   29

1 Samuel

i   29
i 9 f   29
viii 11-16   9
x 12   20
xxii 3   29
xxv   29
xxviii   29

2 Samuel

vii 14   15, 21
viii 18   18
xiv   12, 29
xviii 17b   10
xix 8b   10
xx 1   10

1 Kings

i 29
i 9   34
xi 1   27
xii 16   10
xii 28   34
xv 13   27
xvii 32 f   27
xix 19 f   38
xix 21   39

2 Kings

iii 12   20
vi 21   20
xiii 14   20
xiv 8-14   11
xviii 4   34
xxiii 7   27

Isaiah

i 2   17, 20
i 12-17   12
xxii 21b, 22   17
xxx 9   17 f
xliii 6   23
xliv 9   25
xlvi 3   41
xliv 15   31
l 1   43
lxiii 9b   41
lxiii 16   24
lxiv 7   23 f
lxiv 9   25
lxvi 13   31

Jeremiah

ii 2   44
iii 4, 19   15, 44
vii 17 f   28
xv 10, 17   13
xxx 18   8
xxxi 9   23

Ezekiel

xvi 31
xvi 20   17

Hosea

i-iii   43
ii 4, 7   30
xi 1   23

Zechariah

xii 7   8

Malachi

i 6   15
ii 10   15

Psalms

ii 7   15, 21 ff
xxxiii 6, 7, 9   45
lvii 2   35
lx 5   35
lxiii 8   35
lxviii 6   12
lxxxiii 7   8
lxxxix 21 ff   21
lxxxix 27 f   15
xci 4   35
cii 7 f   13

Job

i 21   33

Proverbs

iii 12   20 f
iii 13-20   4
iv 5   4
viii 22-31   4
viii 27-31   4 f, 44
viii 30   35

Ruth

ii 12   35

Song of Songs   42

Esther   29

Esra-Nehemiah   8

1 Chronicles

xvii 3   21
xxviii 6, 9   15

Sirach
xxiii 1, 4   15
xxv 13-26   5
xxv 24   3
xxvi 1   5
xl 1   34
li 10   16

Sapientia Salomonis
vii 10 ff   4

Judith   29

Philo, de Abrahamo
par. 93   3

4 Maccabees
xv 16, 29   34

Genesis Apocryphon
col. xx, l. 7   3

1 QH ix 35 f   16

b. Bekhorot
fol. 45a   20

b. Pesachim
fol. 66a   20

Matthew
iii 9   24
iii 17   22
x 37   39
xxiii 37   37

Mark
i 11   22
iii 31-35   39

Luke
iii 8   24
iii 22   22
xiii 34   37

John
viii 33   24

Acts
xvii 28   25

1 Corinthians
iv 15b   42

Galatians
iv 19a   42

1 Timothy
ii 11-14   6

b) AUTHORS CITED

Ahlström, G. W.   46
Albright, W. F.   27 f, 34
de Boer, P. A. H.   4 f, 9, 12, 19, 22, 32, 41, 44
Colwell, E. C.   48
Cross, F. M.   27, 31
Curtis, J. B.   27
Daube, D.   7
Donner, H.   16 f
Driver, G. R.   22
Fitzmyer, J. A.   3
Fohrer, G.   38
Gibson, J. C. L.   15
Graham, W. C.   44
Gray, J.   38
Gressmann, H.   27
Guthrie, W. K. C.   23, 36 f
Haeussermann, F.   36
Hamp, V.   5
Hempel, J.   35, 47
Herrmann, W.   32
Holmgren, F.   45
James, E. O.   27, 32
Jastrow, M.   20
Johnson, M. D.   11 f

INDEX

Kapelrud, A. S. 31 f
Kees, H. 39 f
Klengel, H. 9
Koch, K. 8
Kramer, S. N. 15
Kristensen, W. B. 29, 36
Kühlewein, J. 30 f

Lagrange, A. (M.-J.) 24
Lantero, E. H. 5, 38
Leese, K. 41
Levèvre, A. 11
Leipoldt, J. 6
Lidzbarski, M. 16
Löhr, M. 28
Lohse, E. 23

Mace, D. R. 7
Marböck, J. 5
Margulies, H. 32 f
May, H. G. 44
McKane, W. 4
Meek, Th. J. 28
Miller, P. D. 31
Morenz, S. 23
Morgan, J. H. 38
Morgenstern, J. 27

Noyes, M. P. 6

Oppenheim, A. L. 31

Paffrath, P. Th. 22
Patai, R. 27
Pedersen, J. 8, 13

Pilz, E. 27
Plautz, W. 7
Porter, J. R. 8

von Rad, G. 4
Redford, D. B. 19
Reed, W. L. 27
Rilke, R. M. 26
Ringgren, H. 4, 15, 22
Röllig, W. 16 f
Rosenthal, F. 16 f, 40
Rozenberg, M. S. 32

Sauneron, S. 39 f
Schmidt, W. H. 46
Schwally, F. 47
Schweizer, E. 23
Scott, R. B. Y. 5
Sethe, K. 39 f
Smend, R. 28
Soljenitsyn, A. 26
Speiser, E. A. 8
Stade, B. 47

Terrien, S. 33
Thompson, Th. L. 12
Trible, Phyllis 42

Vieyra, M. 40
van den Vondel, J. 3

Weinberg, J. P. 8
Wellhausen, J. 28
Westermann, C. 46

Zandee, J. 39 f